READY, STEADY, PRACTISE!

Frances Naismith

Fractions, Decimals & Percentages
Pupil Book **Year 6**

Features of this book

- Clear explanations and worked examples for each fractions, decimals and percentages topic from the KS2 National Curriculum.

- Questions split into three sections that become progressively more challenging:

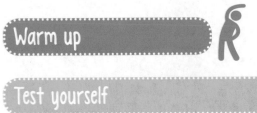

Warm up

Test yourself

Challenge yourself

- 'How did you do?' checks at the end of each topic for self-evaluation.

- Regular progress tests to assess pupils' understanding and recap on their learning.

- Answers to every question in a pull-out section at the centre of the book.

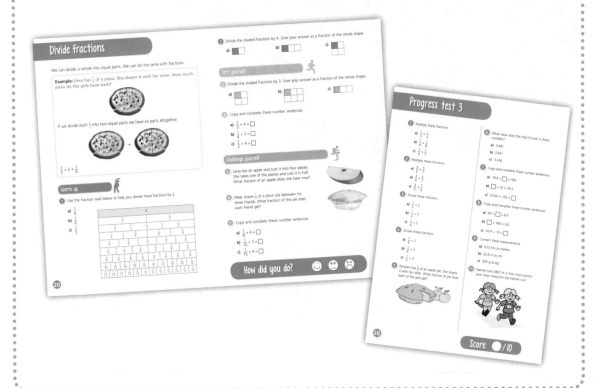

Contents

Simplify fractions

We simplify fractions to make the numerators and denominators as small as possible but when we find equivalent fractions sometimes we go up in size. Simplifying fractions makes them easier to work with.

To simplify, we divide the numerator and denominator by the same number.

Example: Simplify $\frac{5}{15}$.

To simplify $\frac{5}{15}$ we need to find a common factor of both 15 and 5.

5 is a factor of 15 and 5.

We can divide both the numerator and denominator by 5.

$\div 5$

$\frac{5}{15}$ simplifies to $\frac{1}{3}$ $\frac{5}{15} = \frac{1}{3}$ $\frac{5}{15}$ is equivalent to $\frac{1}{3}$

$\div 5$

Warm up

1 Find the lowest common factor for the numerator and denominator in each of these fractions.

a) $\frac{3}{15}$

b) $\frac{8}{16}$

c) $\frac{4}{12}$

2 Copy and complete these number sentences.

a) $\frac{2}{6} = \frac{\boxed{?}}{3}$

b) $\frac{4}{8} = \frac{\boxed{?}}{4}$

c) $\frac{3}{12} = \frac{\boxed{?}}{4}$

3 Find the common factor for the numerator and denominator in each of these fractions.

a) $\frac{9}{12}$

b) $\frac{8}{10}$

c) $\frac{10}{15}$

4 Simplify these fractions to their most simple or lowest form.

a) $\frac{8}{12}$

b) $\frac{10}{18}$

c) $\frac{6}{9}$

Challenge yourself

5 Copy and match the equivalent fractions. One has been done for you.

$\frac{16}{20}$ $\frac{25}{35}$

$\frac{5}{7}$ $\frac{4}{5}$

$\frac{1}{4}$ $\frac{3}{7}$

$\frac{18}{30}$ $\frac{3}{5}$

$\frac{9}{21}$ $\frac{8}{32}$

6 Rav gets $\frac{21}{36}$ for his French test and $\frac{18}{24}$ in his maths test. In which subject did he do best?

7 Simplify these fractions to their most simple or lowest form.

a) $\frac{20}{24}$ b) $\frac{18}{15}$ c) $\frac{12}{30}$

How did you do?

Convert fractions

We can only add or subtract fractions if they have the same denominator. We often need to convert fractions to achieve this.

> **Example:** Convert $\frac{4}{12}$.
>
> We can convert $\frac{4}{12}$ to 6ths or 24ths by dividing or multiplying both the numerator and denominator.
>
> $$\overset{\div 2 \qquad \times 2}{\frac{2}{6} = \frac{4}{12} = \frac{8}{24}}$$
>
> $$\underset{\div 2 \qquad \times 2}{}$$
>
> $\frac{2}{6} = \frac{4}{12} = \frac{8}{24}$

Warm up

1 Convert these fractions to 8ths.

a) $\frac{1}{2}$ b) $\frac{3}{4}$ c) $\frac{1}{4}$

2 Convert these fractions to 12ths.

a) $\frac{1}{6}$ b) $\frac{1}{3}$ c) $\frac{1}{4}$ d) $\frac{1}{2}$

3 Convert these fractions to 20ths.

a) $\frac{1}{5}$ b) $\frac{1}{10}$ c) $\frac{1}{4}$ d) $\frac{1}{2}$

4 Convert these fractions to 16ths.

a) $\frac{1}{2}$ b) $\frac{1}{4}$ c) $\frac{3}{8}$ d) $\frac{7}{8}$

5 Convert these fractions to 10ths.

a) $\frac{3}{5}$ b) $\frac{1}{5}$ c) $\frac{1}{2}$ d) $\frac{4}{5}$

6 Convert these fractions to 24ths.

a) $\dfrac{3}{6}$ **b)** $\dfrac{2}{8}$ **c)** $\dfrac{4}{48}$ **d)** $\dfrac{4}{96}$

7 Convert these fractions to 12ths.

a) $\dfrac{4}{6}$ **b)** $\dfrac{6}{24}$ **c)** $\dfrac{3}{4}$ **d)** $\dfrac{16}{96}$

8 Convert these fractions to 8ths.

a) $\dfrac{3}{4}$ **b)** $\dfrac{1}{2}$ **c)** $\dfrac{6}{16}$ **d)** $\dfrac{16}{32}$

Challenge yourself

9 What denominator would you convert these groups of fractions into before you could work with them?

a) $\dfrac{1}{4}$ $\dfrac{5}{6}$ $\dfrac{7}{12}$

b) $\dfrac{7}{8}$ $\dfrac{19}{24}$ $\dfrac{5}{6}$

c) $\dfrac{3}{5}$ $\dfrac{18}{20}$ $\dfrac{3}{4}$

d) $\dfrac{3}{5}$ $\dfrac{1}{2}$ $\dfrac{7}{10}$

10 Convert these fractions.

a) $\dfrac{4}{6}$ into 12ths and 24ths

b) $\dfrac{6}{8}$ into quarters and 12ths

c) $\dfrac{3}{9}$ into 18ths, 27ths and thirds

How did you do?

Compare fractions

Before we can compare fractions, we need to convert them to the same denominator.

Example: Leo has $\frac{3}{5}$ of a pie and Maya has $\frac{4}{7}$. Who has more pie?

We need to find the lowest common denominator of fifths and sevenths.

The lowest common multiple of 5 and 7 is 35.

We need to convert both fractions to have a denominator of 35.

$$\overset{\times 7}{\frac{3}{5}} = \frac{21}{35} \qquad \overset{\times 5}{\frac{4}{7}} = \frac{20}{35}$$

$$\times 7 \qquad\qquad \times 5$$

$$\frac{21}{35} > \frac{20}{35}$$

So Leo has the most pie.

Warm up

1 Convert each pair of fractions into the same denominator to find out which one is larger.

a) $\frac{4}{5}$ $\frac{7}{15}$

b) $\frac{7}{12}$ $\frac{5}{6}$

c) $\frac{11}{12}$ $\frac{23}{24}$

2 Copy these fraction pairs. Write >, < or = between each pair.

a) $\frac{2}{3} \ \square \ \frac{3}{4}$

b) $\frac{4}{5} \ \square \ \frac{2}{3}$

c) $\frac{3}{4} \ \square \ \frac{5}{6}$

3 Copy these mixed number pairs. Write **>**, **<** or **=** between each pair.

a) $1\frac{3}{5}$ ☐ $1\frac{2}{3}$

b) $2\frac{5}{8}$ ☐ $2\frac{7}{12}$

c) $1\frac{2}{3}$ ☐ $1\frac{5}{8}$

4 Look at these fractions pairs. Which is the smaller fraction in each pair?

a) $\frac{6}{7}$ $\frac{5}{6}$

b) $\frac{4}{5}$ $\frac{6}{8}$

c) $\frac{4}{7}$ $\frac{5}{9}$

Challenge yourself

5 Gina has $\frac{3}{8}$ of a can of cola and Brooklyn has $\frac{7}{12}$.
Who has the most to drink?

6 Laiba has $1\frac{3}{7}$ trays of cookies. Millie has $1\frac{4}{15}$.
Who has more cookies?

7 Write the fraction from inside the circle that
is smaller than the fraction below the circle.

$\frac{4}{6}$ $\frac{3}{4}$

$\frac{3}{5}$ $\frac{1}{2}$

$\frac{3}{4}$ $\frac{4}{6}$

$\frac{3}{10}$ $\frac{6}{7}$

$\frac{3}{4}$ $\frac{5}{6}$

$\frac{4}{5}$ $\frac{1}{2}$

a) $\frac{4}{7}$

b) $\frac{3}{5}$

c) $\frac{6}{8}$

How did you do?

Order fractions

Before we can put fractions in order we need to convert them to all have the same denominator.

We look for the lowest common denominator.

Example: Put $\frac{3}{4}, \frac{2}{3}, \frac{1}{2}$ and $\frac{5}{6}$ in order from the smallest to the largest.

We look for the lowest common multiple of 2, 3, 4 and 6.

The lowest common multiple is 12. The lowest common denominator will be 12ths. We need to convert all the fractions into 12ths.

$$\overset{\times 3}{\frac{3}{4}} = \frac{9}{12} \qquad \overset{\times 4}{\frac{2}{3}} = \frac{8}{12} \qquad \overset{\times 6}{\frac{1}{2}} = \frac{6}{12} \qquad \overset{\times 2}{\frac{5}{6}} = \frac{10}{12}$$
$$\underset{\times 3}{} \qquad \underset{\times 4}{} \qquad \underset{\times 6}{} \qquad \underset{\times 2}{}$$

We can now put the fractions in order from smallest to largest:

$$\frac{1}{2} \qquad \frac{2}{3} \qquad \frac{3}{4} \qquad \frac{5}{6}$$

Warm up

1. Write these fractions in order from smallest to largest. You will need to find the lowest common denominator first.

    a) $\frac{1}{2}$ $\quad$ $\frac{3}{4}$ $\quad$ $\frac{5}{8}$

    b) $\frac{5}{6}$ $\quad$ $\frac{2}{3}$ $\quad$ $\frac{1}{2}$

    c) $\frac{2}{3}$ $\quad$ $\frac{1}{4}$ $\quad$ $\frac{2}{6}$ $\quad$ $\frac{5}{12}$

2. Write these fractions in order from smallest to largest. You will need to convert them first.

    a) $\frac{2}{5}$ $\quad$ $\frac{6}{10}$ $\quad$ $\frac{1}{2}$

    b) $\frac{3}{16}$ $\quad$ $\frac{3}{4}$ $\quad$ $\frac{3}{8}$

    c) $\frac{4}{12}$ $\quad$ $\frac{5}{6}$ $\quad$ $\frac{6}{24}$

3 Write the fractions in the circles in order from smallest to largest.

a)
$\dfrac{5}{6}$ $\dfrac{3}{4}$
$\dfrac{2}{3}$ $\dfrac{1}{2}$

b)
$\dfrac{5}{8}$ $\dfrac{2}{6}$
$\dfrac{2}{3}$ $\dfrac{1}{2}$

c)
$\dfrac{2}{6}$
$\dfrac{3}{4}$ $\dfrac{2}{3}$
$\dfrac{7}{8}$ $\dfrac{5}{12}$

Challenge yourself

4 Write these fractions in order from smallest to largest.

a) $1\dfrac{5}{12}$ $1\dfrac{3}{8}$ $\dfrac{11}{12}$ $\dfrac{3}{4}$ $1\dfrac{5}{6}$ $\dfrac{1}{2}$ $1\dfrac{2}{3}$

b) $1\dfrac{1}{3}$ $1\dfrac{5}{6}$ $2\dfrac{1}{2}$ $\dfrac{6}{7}$ $1\dfrac{5}{14}$ $\dfrac{20}{21}$

c) $\dfrac{28}{24}$ $\dfrac{7}{12}$ $\dfrac{14}{8}$ $\dfrac{6}{3}$ $\dfrac{6}{4}$ $\dfrac{10}{6}$

How did you do?

Add fractions

We can add fractions with the same denominators.

$$\frac{5}{9} + \frac{3}{9} = \frac{8}{9}$$

$$\frac{4}{5} + \frac{3}{5} = \frac{7}{5} = 1\frac{2}{5}$$

To add fractions with different denominators we need to find the lowest common multiple of the denominators.

Example: Add $\frac{1}{3} + \frac{1}{4}$.

The lowest common multiple of 3 and 4 is 12.

We need to convert both fractions to 12ths.

$$\frac{1}{3} = \frac{4}{12} \qquad \frac{1}{4} = \frac{3}{12}$$

$$\frac{4}{12} + \frac{3}{12} = \frac{7}{12}$$

$$\frac{1}{3} + \frac{1}{4} = \frac{7}{12}$$

Warm up

1 Add these fractions.

   a) $\frac{3}{4} + \frac{1}{8}$

   b) $\frac{1}{6} + \frac{1}{3}$

   c) $\frac{1}{5} + \frac{1}{10}$

2 Add these fractions.

   a) $\frac{1}{6} + \frac{2}{3}$

   b) $\frac{2}{8} + \frac{3}{4}$

   c) $\frac{1}{6} + \frac{4}{12}$

$3+5=8$

3 Add these fractions.

a) $\frac{1}{12} + \frac{1}{4} + \frac{1}{6}$

b) $\frac{1}{8} + \frac{1}{4} + \frac{1}{2}$

c) $\frac{1}{3} + \frac{1}{6} + \frac{1}{12}$

4 Add these fractions, giving your answers as mixed numbers.

a) $\frac{5}{6} + \frac{7}{8}$

b) $\frac{7}{8} + \frac{5}{12}$

c) $\frac{4}{5} + \frac{2}{3}$

Challenge yourself

5 Add these fractions, simplifying your answers where possible.

a) $\frac{2}{7} + \frac{3}{6}$

b) $\frac{4}{12} + \frac{5}{30}$

c) $\frac{2}{5} + \frac{2}{7}$

6 Gill has $\frac{2}{5}$ of a cheesecake, Rav has $\frac{1}{4}$ and Jack has $\frac{1}{3}$. How much cheesecake do the children have altogether?

7 Mia has three fraction cards. What is the total of her fractions?

$$\frac{2}{9} \qquad \frac{1}{6} \qquad \frac{1}{4}$$

How did you do?

Subtract fractions

We can subtract fractions with the same denominators.

$$\frac{5}{9} - \frac{3}{9} = \frac{2}{9}$$

$$1\frac{4}{5} - \frac{3}{5} = 1\frac{1}{5}$$

To subtract fractions with different denominators we need to find the lowest common multiple of the denominators.

Example: What is $\frac{1}{3} - \frac{1}{5}$?

The lowest common multiple of 3 and 5 is 15.

We need to convert both fractions to 15ths.

$$\frac{1}{3} = \frac{5}{15} \qquad \frac{1}{5} = \frac{3}{15}$$

$$\frac{5}{15} - \frac{3}{15} = \frac{2}{15}$$

$$\frac{1}{3} - \frac{1}{5} = \frac{2}{15}$$

Warm up

1 Subtract these fractions.

a) $\frac{3}{4} - \frac{1}{2}$

b) $\frac{5}{8} - \frac{1}{4}$

c) $\frac{4}{10} - \frac{1}{20}$

2 Subtract these fractions.

a) $\frac{5}{6} - \frac{2}{3}$

b) $\frac{10}{12} - \frac{3}{4}$

c) $\frac{4}{5} - \frac{2}{10}$

3 Subtract these mixed numbers.

a) $1\frac{3}{4} - 1\frac{3}{8}$

b) $2\frac{5}{6} - 1\frac{2}{12}$

c) $1\frac{8}{12} - 1\frac{1}{3}$

d) $1\frac{1}{2} - 1\frac{1}{3}$

e) $2\frac{1}{8} - 1\frac{1}{4}$

f) $1\frac{10}{15} - 1\frac{1}{5}$

Challenge yourself

4 Subtract these fractions, simplifying your answers where possible.

a) $\frac{11}{12} - \frac{1}{3} - \frac{1}{4}$

b) $\frac{14}{15} - \frac{2}{5} - \frac{1}{3}$

c) $\frac{18}{24} - \frac{2}{6} - \frac{4}{12}$

5 Leo and Ibrahim share a pizza. Leo eats $\frac{5}{8}$, Ibrahim eats $\frac{2}{12}$. How much pizza is left?

6 Ruby, Alex and Hassan are emptying the fish tank. Ruby pours out $\frac{1}{6}$, Alex takes out $\frac{2}{7}$ and Hassan pours away $\frac{1}{3}$ of the water. How much water is left?

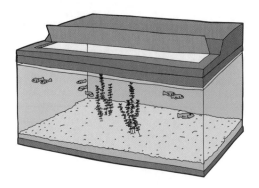

How did you do?

1 Simplify these fractions.

a) $\frac{5}{20}$

b) $\frac{11}{33}$

c) $\frac{12}{48}$

2 Simplify these fractions.

a) $\frac{27}{30}$

b) $\frac{26}{48}$

c) $\frac{36}{60}$

3 Convert these fractions to thirds.

a) $\frac{8}{12}$

b) $\frac{4}{6}$

c) $\frac{9}{27}$

4 Convert these fractions to sixths.

a) $\frac{10}{12}$

b) $\frac{1}{3}$

c) $\frac{16}{48}$

5 Copy these pairs and circle the smaller fraction from each pair.

a) $\frac{12}{15}$ $\frac{3}{7}$

b) $\frac{16}{12}$ $\frac{14}{7}$

c) $\frac{9}{12}$ $\frac{14}{20}$

6 Mia and Tabitha each have a fraction card. Whose fraction is the largest?

Mia   **$\frac{12}{30}$**   Tabitha   **$\frac{18}{40}$**

7 Order these fractions from smallest to largest.

$\frac{8}{12}$ $\frac{5}{6}$ $\frac{1}{2}$ $\frac{3}{4}$ $\frac{4}{12}$

8 Order these fractions from smallest to largest.

$\frac{7}{12}$ $\frac{4}{6}$ $\frac{5}{8}$ $\frac{3}{4}$

9 Ollie has $\frac{2}{7}$ of a tray of toffee. Luca has $\frac{1}{6}$ of the tray. How much toffee do the children have altogether?

10 Dylan makes a tray of 24 brownies. He gives away $\frac{3}{8}$ of his brownies. What fraction of his tray does he have left?

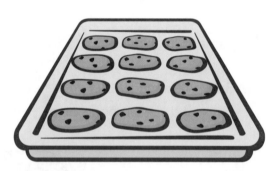

Score ⬤/10

1 Simplify these fractions.

   a) $\dfrac{30}{105}$

   b) $\dfrac{78}{104}$

   c) $\dfrac{20}{35}$

2 Convert these fractions to 12ths.

   a) $\dfrac{2}{4}$

   b) $\dfrac{4}{48}$

   c) $\dfrac{16}{96}$

3 Muhammad got $\dfrac{12}{24}$ in his science test and $\dfrac{18}{30}$ in his maths test.
   In which subject did Muhammad do best?

4 Order these fraction cards from smallest to largest.

   $\dfrac{14}{20}$ $\dfrac{3}{5}$ $\dfrac{18}{40}$ $\dfrac{5}{8}$ $\dfrac{2}{10}$

5 Add these fraction cards.

   $\dfrac{5}{24}$ $\dfrac{3}{8}$ $\dfrac{1}{6}$

6 Nur has $\dfrac{3}{10}$ of a bottle of water. Connor adds $\dfrac{7}{15}$.
   How much water do the children have altogether?

7 $\dfrac{6}{7} - \dfrac{3}{4} = ?$

8 Ava has a jug of lemonade. She pours out $\dfrac{2}{5}$ of it and then another $\dfrac{5}{15}$.
   How much lemonade is left?

9 Simplify these fractions.

   a) $\dfrac{12}{32}$

   b) $\dfrac{15}{105}$

   c) $\dfrac{16}{56}$

10 What is the lowest common denominator for these fractions?

   $\dfrac{1}{7}$ $\dfrac{1}{5}$ $\dfrac{1}{4}$

Score ⬤/10

Multiply fractions

To multiply fractions we multiply the **numerators** and the **denominators**.

$$\frac{1}{3} \times \frac{1}{4} = \frac{1 \times 1}{3 \times 4} = \frac{1}{12}$$

Example: What is $\frac{3}{4} \times \frac{2}{3}$?

$$\frac{3 \times 2}{4 \times 3}$$

$$= \frac{6}{12} \qquad \text{This can be simplified}$$

$$= \frac{1}{2}$$

Example: What is $\frac{1}{2} \times \frac{1}{4} \times \frac{1}{3}$?

$$\frac{1 \times 1 \times 1}{2 \times 4 \times 3}$$

$$= \frac{1}{24}$$

Warm up

1 Multiply these fractions.

a) $\frac{1}{4} \times \frac{1}{2}$

b) $\frac{1}{3} \times \frac{1}{5}$

c) $\frac{1}{6} \times \frac{1}{4}$

2 Multiply these fractions.

a) $\frac{2}{3} \times \frac{3}{5}$

b) $\frac{4}{7} \times \frac{2}{3}$

c) $\frac{3}{4} \times \frac{5}{6}$

3 Multiply these fractions.

a) $\frac{1}{3} \times \frac{5}{7}$

b) $\frac{3}{7} \times \frac{5}{4}$

c) $\frac{7}{5} \times \frac{3}{4}$

4 Multiply these fractions, simplifying your answers.

a) $\frac{2}{6} \times \frac{3}{4}$

b) $\frac{5}{7} \times \frac{2}{5}$

c) $\frac{3}{4} \times \frac{6}{8}$

Challenge yourself

5 Multiply these fraction cards.

a) $\frac{2}{5}$ $\frac{3}{12}$ $\frac{4}{3}$

b) $\frac{3}{4}$ $\frac{3}{8}$ $\frac{5}{6}$

c) $\frac{2}{3}$ $\frac{4}{7}$ $\frac{5}{8}$

6 Copy and complete these number sentences.

a) $\frac{2}{3} \times \frac{\square}{6} = \frac{8}{\square}$

b) $\frac{\square}{8} \times \frac{5}{\square} = \frac{10}{48}$

c) $\frac{5}{\square} \times \frac{4}{9} = \frac{\square}{36}$

How did you do?

Divide fractions

We can divide a whole into equal parts. We can do the same with fractions.

Example: Uma has $\frac{1}{3}$ of a pizza. She shares it with her sister. How much pizza do the girls have each?

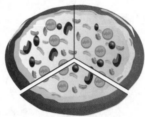

If we divide each $\frac{1}{3}$ into two equal parts we have six parts altogether.

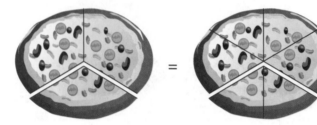

$$\frac{1}{3} \div 2 = \frac{1}{6}$$

Warm up

1. Use the fraction wall below to help you divide these fractions by 2.

a) $\frac{1}{4}$

b) $\frac{1}{6}$

c) $\frac{1}{5}$

1											
$\frac{1}{2}$						$\frac{1}{2}$					
$\frac{1}{3}$				$\frac{1}{3}$				$\frac{1}{3}$			
$\frac{1}{4}$			$\frac{1}{4}$			$\frac{1}{4}$			$\frac{1}{4}$		
$\frac{1}{5}$		$\frac{1}{5}$		$\frac{1}{5}$		$\frac{1}{5}$		$\frac{1}{5}$			
$\frac{1}{6}$		$\frac{1}{6}$		$\frac{1}{6}$		$\frac{1}{6}$		$\frac{1}{6}$		$\frac{1}{6}$	
$\frac{1}{8}$	$\frac{1}{8}$	$\frac{1}{8}$	$\frac{1}{8}$	$\frac{1}{8}$	$\frac{1}{8}$	$\frac{1}{8}$	$\frac{1}{8}$				
$\frac{1}{10}$	$\frac{1}{10}$	$\frac{1}{10}$	$\frac{1}{10}$	$\frac{1}{10}$	$\frac{1}{10}$	$\frac{1}{10}$	$\frac{1}{10}$	$\frac{1}{10}$	$\frac{1}{10}$		
$\frac{1}{12}$	$\frac{1}{12}$	$\frac{1}{12}$	$\frac{1}{12}$	$\frac{1}{12}$	$\frac{1}{12}$	$\frac{1}{12}$	$\frac{1}{12}$	$\frac{1}{12}$	$\frac{1}{12}$	$\frac{1}{12}$	$\frac{1}{12}$

2 Divide the shaded fractions by 4. Give your answer as a fraction of the whole shape.

a)

b)

c)

Test yourself

3 Divide the shaded fractions by 3. Give your answer as a fraction of the whole shape.

a)

b)

c)

4 Copy and complete these number sentences.

a) $\frac{1}{3} \div 4 = \square$

b) $\frac{1}{4} \div 3 = \square$

c) $\frac{1}{2} \div 4 = \square$

Challenge yourself

5 Lena has an apple and cuts it into four pieces. She takes one of the pieces and cuts it in half. What fraction of an apple does she have now?

6 Peter shares $\frac{1}{3}$ of a plum pie between his three friends. What fraction of the pie does each friend get?

7 Copy and complete these number sentences.

a) $\frac{1}{8} \div 4 = \square$

b) $\frac{1}{10} \div 3 = \square$

c) $\frac{1}{15} \div 4 = \square$

How did you do?

You can tell the value of a number by looking at the position of its digits.

$$U . \frac{1}{10} \quad \frac{1}{100} \quad \frac{1}{1000}$$

$$1 . 3 \quad 5 \quad 2$$

This number has 1 unit   (1)

3 tenths   (0.3)

5 hundredths   (0.05)

2 thousandths   (0.002)

If we divide one whole into ten we get tenths or $\frac{1}{10}$.

If we divide $\frac{1}{10}$ into ten we get hundredths or $\frac{1}{100}$.

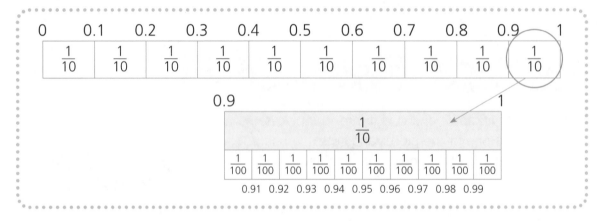

If we divide $\frac{1}{100}$ into ten we get thousandths or $\frac{1}{1000}$.

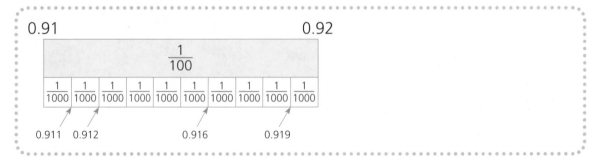

1 What is the value of the digit 3 in these decimals?

a) 1.345   **b)** 1.543   **c)** 1.435

2 What decimals are at **a**, **b**, **c** and **d** on the number line?

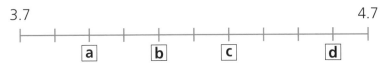

3 Write a number with:

a) 4 hundredths

b) 7 tenths

c) 2 thousandths

4 What decimals are at **a**, **b**, **c** and **d** on the number line?

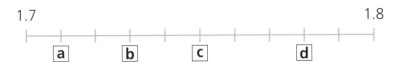

5 Write a number with:

a) three tenths, five hundredths and two units

b) four thousandths, six tenths, and eight hundredths

c) nine thousandths, no tenths and three hundredths

6 What decimals are at **a**, **b**, **c** and **d** on the number line?

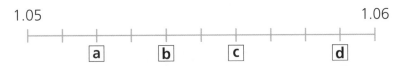

How did you do?

Multiply by 10, 100 and 1000

Each time we multiply numbers by 10, the digits move one place to the left.

Example: Multiply 0.436 × 10, 100 and 1000.

×10	×100	×1000

H T U. $\frac{1}{10}$ $\frac{1}{100}$ $\frac{1}{1000}$

0 . 4   3   6

⟵ 4 . 3   6

moves one place to the left

H T U. $\frac{1}{10}$ $\frac{1}{100}$ $\frac{1}{1000}$

0 . 4   3   6

4 3 . 6 ⟵

moves two places to the left

H T U. $\frac{1}{10}$ $\frac{1}{100}$ $\frac{1}{1000}$

0 . 4   3   6

4 3 6 ⟵

moves three places to the left

Warm up

1 Multiply these numbers by 10.

   a) 25

   b) 3.2

   c) 0.5

2 Multiply these numbers by 100.

   a) 0.76

   b) 7.4

   c) 0.062

3 Multiply these numbers by 1000.

   a) 0.759

   b) 0.613

   c) 0.542

4 Multiply these numbers by 10.

    a) 2.7

    b) 3.45

    c) 9.567

5 Multiply these numbers by 100.

    a) 5.4

    b) 8.734

    c) 5.07

6 Multiply these numbers by 1000.

    a) 23.5

    b) 0.003

    c) 9.54

Challenge yourself

7 Copy and complete these number sentences.

    a) $4.52 \times \square = 452$

    b) $\square \times 1000 = 30.5$

    c) $0.006 \times 100 = \square$

8 Sajid runs 5.456 km. How many metres does Sajid run?

9 Poppy has some plastic bricks. Each brick is 3.42 cm long.
Poppy joins 100 bricks together. How long is Poppy's line of bricks in cm?

How did you do?

Divide by 10, 100 and 1000

Each time we divide numbers by 10, the digits move one place to the right.

Example: 736 ÷ 10, 100 and 1000.

÷ 10	÷ 100	÷ 1000
H T U . $\frac{1}{10}$ $\frac{1}{100}$ $\frac{1}{1000}$ 7 3 6 ⟶ 7 3 . 6 moves one place to the right	H T U . $\frac{1}{10}$ $\frac{1}{100}$ $\frac{1}{1000}$ 7 3 6 ⟶ 7 . 3 6 moves two places to the right	H T U . $\frac{1}{10}$ $\frac{1}{100}$ $\frac{1}{1000}$ 7 3 6 ⟶ 0 . 7 3 6 moves three places to the right

Warm up

1 Divide these numbers by 10.

 a) 5

 b) 3

 c) 7

2 Divide these numbers by 100.

 a) 43

 b) 86

 c) 52

3 Divide these numbers by 1000.

 a) 546

 b) 238

 c) 967

4 Divide these numbers by 10.

   a) 680

   b) 95

   c) 0.48

5 Divide these numbers by 100.

   a) 564

   b) 31.8

   c) 476

6 Divide these numbers by 1000.

   a) 5246

   b) 2738

   c) 4567

Challenge yourself

7 Copy and complete these number sentences.

   a) 76 ÷ ☐ = 0.76

   b) ☐ ÷ 1000 = 0.27

   c) 56 ÷ 100 = ☐

8 Easha has 34.5 m of ribbon. She cuts it into 1000 equal pieces. How long is each piece?

9 Daniel counts all the pennies in the jar.
How much money does Daniel have in pounds?

4573p

How did you do?

1 Multiply these fractions.

 a) $\frac{1}{3} \times \frac{1}{5}$

 b) $\frac{1}{4} \times \frac{1}{8}$

 c) $\frac{1}{9} \times \frac{1}{7}$

2 Multiply these fractions.

 a) $\frac{3}{6} \times \frac{5}{7}$

 b) $\frac{3}{4} \times \frac{5}{7}$

 c) $\frac{3}{5} \times \frac{7}{6}$

3 Divide these fractions.

 a) $\frac{1}{5} \div 2$

 b) $\frac{1}{3} \div 3$

 c) $\frac{1}{4} \div 5$

4 Divide these fractions.

 a) $\frac{1}{8} \div 2$

 b) $\frac{1}{4} \div 3$

 c) $\frac{1}{7} \div 3$

5 Parveen has $\frac{1}{3}$ of an apple pie. She shares it with her sister. What fraction of pie does each of the girls get?

6 What value does the digit 8 have in these numbers?

 a) 3.481

 b) 3.841

 c) 3.418

7 Copy and complete these number sentences.

 a) $78.9 \times \square = 789$

 b) $\square \times 10 = 34.5$

 c) $0.003 \times 100 = \square$

8 Copy and complete these number sentences.

 a) $84 \div \square = 8.4$

 b) $\square \div 100 = 3.6$

 c) $43.9 \div 10 = \square$

9 Convert these measurements.

 a) 23.5 km to metres

 b) 32.8 m to cm

 c) 655 g to kg

10 Harriet runs 3457 m in the cross country race. How many km has Harriet run?

Score ◯/10

1 Multiply these fractions, simplifying your answers.

a) $\frac{2}{5} \times \frac{3}{6}$

b) $\frac{5}{8} \times \frac{6}{7}$

c) $\frac{4}{9} \times \frac{6}{8}$

2 Azan has $\frac{1}{5}$ of a bottle of cola. He shares it equally with his two friends. How much does each of the three children have?

3 Complete these number sentences.

a) $\frac{1}{\square} \div 3 = \frac{1}{9}$

b) $\frac{2}{\square} \times \frac{\square}{4} = \frac{6}{16}$

c) $\frac{\square}{4} \div \square = \frac{1}{8}$

4 Look at the number **2.317**. Which digit has the following value?

a) hundredths

b) tenths

c) thousandths

5 Copy and complete these number sentences.

a) $0.022 \times \square = 2.2$

b) $\square \div 1000 = 2.36$

c) $0.8 \div 100 = \square$

6 Elana has 45 metres of rope. She cuts it into 100 equal pieces. How long is each piece in metres?

7 Keira has 100 wooden bricks. Each brick is 3.25 cm long. If Keira places the bricks end to end, how long is her line of bricks in cm?

8 Write a number with no units, three hundredths, no tenths and five thousandths.

9 Convert £78.95 to pence.

10 Angus has 46.3 metres of fishing line. He cuts it into 10 equal pieces. How long is each piece?

Multiply decimals

We often need to multiply decimals in money problems.

Example: Tom gets £5.35 pocket money each week. How much money will Tom have after 12 weeks?

We start by multiplying the £5.35 by the units digit as we would for normal long multiplication. We continue by multiplying by the tens digit, not forgetting our place holder. We can ignore the decimal point.

```
   5.3 5
 ×  1,2
 1 0 7 0
 5 3,5 0
 6 4 2 0
```
←———— We add our figures to get a total

```
   5.(3 5)
 ×  1,2
 1 0 7 0
 5 3,5 0
 6 4.2 0
```

There are two digits after the decimal place in our question so we need to have two digits after the decimal place in our answer

We insert the decimal point in the correct place in our answer

£5.35 × 12 = £64.20

1 Use the method in the example box above to complete these calculations.

a) 4.5 × 7

b) 5.3 × 8

c) 7.6 × 5

30

2 Use the method in the example box on page 30 to complete these calculations.

a) 3.65 × 6

b) 4.53 × 6

c) 8.17 × 5

Challenge yourself

3 Use the method in the example box on page 30 to complete these calculations.

a) 3.68 × 38

b) 4.84 × 57

c) 3.67 × 69

4 Dictionaries cost £7.65 each. Mrs Smart buys 24 for her Year 6 class. How much does Mrs Smart spend altogether?

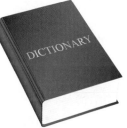

5 Roopa saves £3.25 every week for 25 weeks. How much money has she saved altogether?

6 Darren and George want to buy fish and chips for their party. If each portion costs £6.45, how much money will the boys need if 21 people come to the party?

How did you do?

Divide giving decimal answers

We can use the bus-stop method of division to divide a number.

Example 1: Divide 114 by 8.

$114 \div 8 = 14 \text{ r } 2$

$$\begin{array}{r} 0\ 1\ 4 \\ \hline 8\ \overline{|\ 1\ 1^3\ 4^2} \end{array}$$

We are left with a remainder of 2

$$\begin{array}{r} 0\ 1\ 4. \\ \hline 8\ \overline{|\ 1\ 1^3\ 4.^{20}} \end{array}$$

We can add a decimal point and make our 2 into 20 tenths

8 into 20 is 2 with a remainder of 4.

$$\begin{array}{r} 0\ 1\ 4.2\ 5 \\ \hline 8\ \overline{|\ 1\ 1^3\ 4.20^{40}} \end{array}$$

We can make our remainder 4 into 0.040

8 into 40 is 5

$114 \div 8 = 14.25$

Sometimes when we divide numbers we continue to get the same answer. This is called a recurring decimal. The answer needs to be shortened to one or two decimal places using rounding (see page 36).

$$\begin{array}{r} 0\ 3.3\ 3\ 3\ 3 \\ \hline 3\ \overline{|\ 1\ 0^{10\ 10\ 10}} \end{array}$$

We often need to divide decimals when we are solving problems involving money.

Example 2: Divide 34.65 by 5.

$34 \div 5 = 6 \text{ remainder } 4$

$$\begin{array}{r} 6.9\ 3 \\ \hline 5\ \overline{|\ 3\ 4.^4 6^1\ 5} \end{array}$$

We can't divide 4 by 5 so we put a decimal point on our answer line

$\dfrac{46}{5} = 9 \text{ r } 1$

$\dfrac{15}{5} = 3$

1. Use the method in the example box on page 32 to complete these division calculations.

   a) 78 ÷ 6   **b)** 136 ÷ 5   **c)** 147 ÷ 6   **d)** 44 ÷ 5

Test yourself

2. Use the method in the example box on page 32 to complete these division calculations.

   a) 66 ÷ 8

   b) 105 ÷ 4

   c) 138 ÷ 8

   d) 58 ÷ 8

Challenge yourself

3. Use the method in the example box on page 32 to complete these division calculations.

   a) 386 ÷ 8

   b) 205 ÷ 4

   c) 354 ÷ 8

4. Lucy is making 12 bowls of fruit salad for the school canteen. She has 99 apples. How many apples will go into each bowl?

5. Sui has 256 books. If she puts 8 books on each shelf in the library, how many shelves will she need?

How did you do?

Calculate decimal fractions

We can convert simple fractions to decimals using division.

Example: What is $\frac{3}{8}$ as a decimal?

We know that $\frac{3}{8}$ means $3 \div 8$

We can use the bus-stop method to divide.

$$8 \overline{)3^0}$$
$$0$$

We cannot divide 3 by 8 so we record a zero

$$8 \overline{)3^0{}^{60}}$$
$$0.3$$

We add a decimal point

$30 \div 8 = 3$ remainder 6

$$8 \overline{)3^{30}{}^{60}{}^4}$$
$$0.37$$

$60 \div 8 = 7$ remainder 4

$$8 \overline{)3^{30}{}^{60}{}^{40}}$$
$$0.375$$

$40 \div 8 = 5$

$\frac{3}{8} = 3 \div 8$

$= 0.375$

Warm up

1. Convert these fractions to decimals using the bus-stop method.

   a) $\frac{1}{5}$

   b) $\frac{1}{4}$

   c) $\frac{3}{5}$

   d) $\frac{1}{2}$

   e) $\frac{3}{10}$

   f) $\frac{4}{5}$

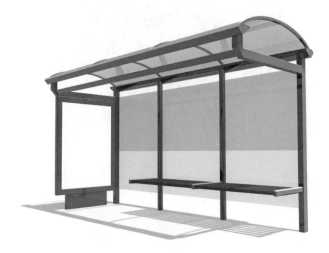

2) Convert these fractions to decimals using the bus-stop method.

a) $\frac{3}{4}$

b) $\frac{5}{8}$

c) $\frac{2}{8}$

Challenge yourself

3) Convert these fractions to decimals using the bus-stop method.

a) $\frac{6}{16}$

b) $\frac{7}{4}$

c) $\frac{9}{8}$

4) Match each fraction to its decimal equivalent.

$\frac{1}{4}$ **0.5**

$\frac{2}{5}$ **0.4**

$\frac{1}{8}$ **0.25**

$\frac{2}{4}$ **0.125**

How did you do?

Rounding decimals

We round numbers to make them easier to communicate, to gain an estimate or to check if the answer is sensible.

The rules for rounding decimals are the same as those for rounding whole numbers.

Example: Round 3.485.

To the nearest whole number	To the nearest one decimal place	To the nearest two decimal places
To round 3.485 to the nearest whole number we look at the tenths column. It's a 4 so we round down to 3	To round 3.485 to one decimal place we look at the hundredths column. It's an 8 so we round up to 3.5	To round 3.485 to two decimal places we look at the thousandths column. It's a 5 so we round up to 3.49

Warm up

1. Round these decimals to one decimal place.

   a) 6.32

   b) 7.29

   c) 24.81

2. Add these decimals and round your answers to the nearest whole number.

   a) 12.4 + 16.9

   b) 24.5 + 23.1

   c) 17.8 + 25.6

3 Which of the estimated answers below gives the nearest answer to 6.8 × 3.4 rounded?

18   18.32   21   24

4 Multiply these decimals and round your answers to the nearest one decimal place.

a) 2.43 × 6

b) 5 × 6.61

c) 3.68 × 9

Challenge yourself

5 Round the answer to these calculations.

a) 1234 m + 4932 m to the nearest km.

b) £25.49 − £18.76 to the nearest pound.

c) 67 cm × 8 to the nearest metre.

6 What is the perimeter of this regular shape? Give your answer to the nearest one decimal place.

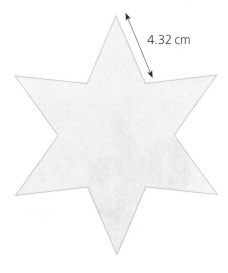

4.32 cm

How did you do?

Fractions, decimals and percentages

We need to know the decimal and percentage equivalents for common fractions.

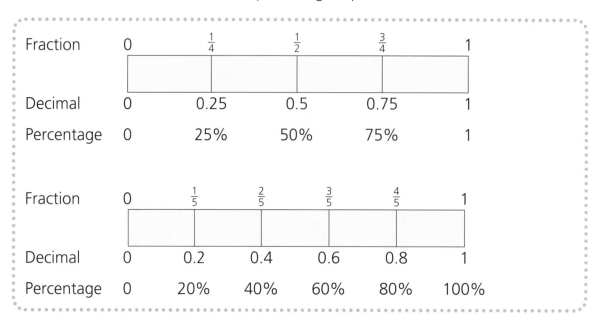

Fraction	0	$\frac{1}{4}$	$\frac{1}{2}$	$\frac{3}{4}$	1
Decimal	0	0.25	0.5	0.75	1
Percentage	0	25%	50%	75%	1

Fraction	0	$\frac{1}{5}$	$\frac{2}{5}$	$\frac{3}{5}$	$\frac{4}{5}$	1
Decimal	0	0.2	0.4	0.6	0.8	1
Percentage	0	20%	40%	60%	80%	100%

Knowing these equivalents helps us to compare them.

Example: Which is bigger, $\frac{24}{30}$ or 75%?

$\frac{24}{30}$

$= \frac{8}{10}$

$= \frac{80}{100}$

$= 80\%$

80% > 75%

$\frac{24}{30} > 75\%$

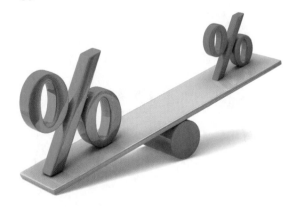

1 Convert these fractions to decimals.

a) $\frac{2}{5}$

b) $\frac{6}{8}$

c) $\frac{3}{12}$

2 Convert these fractions to percentages.

a) $\frac{1}{20}$

b) $\frac{1}{50}$

c) $\frac{1}{25}$

Test yourself

3 Convert these fractions to percentages.

a) $\frac{8}{40}$ b) $\frac{27}{30}$ c) $\frac{63}{90}$

4 Copy and complete these number sentences.

a) $\frac{4}{5} = \square\%$

b) $0.32 = \frac{\square}{\square}$

c) $0.45 = \square\%$

Challenge yourself

5 Write **>**, **<** or **=** between these amounts.

a) $30\% \square \frac{12}{20}$

b) $0.125 \square \frac{1}{8}$

c) $\frac{8}{24} \square 35\%$

6 Leo got 45% in a test. Gina got $\frac{8}{12}$. Who scored the highest?

How did you do?

1 3.45 × 9 = ?

2 Madame Chou-Chou buys 26 French dictionaries for her class. Each dictionary costs £3.46. How much does she spend altogether?

3 Granny Emily saves £24. She shares it between her 5 grandchildren. How much do the children get each?

4 279 ÷ 15 = ?

5 Convert these fractions to decimals.

a) $\frac{6}{8}$

b) $\frac{9}{12}$

c) $\frac{4}{16}$

6 Match these decimals and fractions.

0.01		$\frac{6}{8}$
0.50		$\frac{3}{24}$
0.75		$\frac{1}{100}$
0.125		$\frac{12}{24}$

7 12.45 + 17.68 = ?
Round your answer to one decimal place.

8 4.6 × 5 = ?
Round your answer to one decimal place.

9 Fill in the blanks in this number sentence.

$80\% = 0.\square = \dfrac{\square}{\square} = \dfrac{\square}{\square}$

10 Harry gets $\frac{15}{20}$ in a test. Toby gets 70%. Who has the highest score?

Score ⬤ / 10

1 8.1 × 34 = ?

2 Mike buys 12 CDs. Each CD costs £7.45. How much does Mike spend?

3 174 ÷ 8 = ?

4 Liam cuts 438 metres of string into 24 equal pieces. How long is each piece?

5 Dylan has $\frac{5}{8}$ of a pizza. What is this fraction as a decimal?

6 34.675 − 12.531 = ?
Round your answer to two decimal places.

7 7.9 × 24 = ?
Round your answer to the nearest whole number.

8 Abbie scores $\frac{12}{20}$ in her science test and $\frac{16}{25}$ in her maths test. In which test did Abbie do best?

9 Match the equivalent fractions, decimals and percentages.

12.5%	0.035
0.35	$\frac{3}{12}$
25%	$\frac{70}{200}$
$\frac{35}{1000}$	0.125

10 Copy and complete this number sentence.

$$\boxed{}\% = 0.25 = \frac{\boxed{}}{\boxed{}} = \frac{\boxed{}}{\boxed{}}$$

Score ⬤ /10

41

Mixed test

1 Simplify these fractions.

a) $\dfrac{350}{1000}$

b) $\dfrac{24}{56}$

c) $\dfrac{12}{90}$

2 Convert these fractions to the same denominator.

$\dfrac{3}{4}$ $\qquad$ $\dfrac{5}{6}$ $\qquad$ $\dfrac{7}{8}$

3 Circle the smaller fraction in each pair.

a) 0.25 $\qquad$ $\dfrac{1}{3}$

b) $\dfrac{7}{10}$ $\qquad$ 0.75

c) 0.3 $\qquad$ $\dfrac{2}{5}$

4 Put these fractions on order from smallest to largest.

$\dfrac{2}{3}$ $\qquad$ $\dfrac{3}{4}$ $\qquad$ $\dfrac{7}{12}$ $\qquad$ $\dfrac{5}{6}$ $\qquad$ $\dfrac{1}{2}$

5 Emily has $\dfrac{2}{5}$ of a chocolate cake, Esther has $\dfrac{6}{15}$ and Tanisha has $\dfrac{7}{10}$. How much cake do the girls have altogether?

6 Copy and complete this number sentence.

$\dfrac{1}{4} + \dfrac{3}{\square} = \dfrac{5}{\square}$

7 Annette has an apple pie. She keeps $\dfrac{1}{6}$ of the pie for herself and gives away $\dfrac{1}{4}$ of it. How much pie is left in the dish?

8 Multiply these fraction cards.

$\dfrac{2}{3}$ $\qquad$ $\dfrac{1}{4}$ $\qquad$ $\dfrac{1}{2}$

9 $\frac{1}{5} \div 3 = ?$

10 Liam has $\frac{1}{4}$ of a raspberry tart. He shares it equally with his brother. How much tart does each boy get?

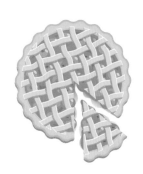

11 $2\frac{4}{\square} + \frac{\square}{11} = 2\frac{7}{\square}$

12 Convert $\frac{7}{8}$ to a decimal.

13 What value does the digit 2 have in the number 3.452?

14 Which digit show the number of tenths in 56.73?

15 Copy and complete this number sentence.

$\square \div 100 = 0.543$

16 Jo earns £8.75 for each car she washes. Jo washes 12 cars. How much money does she earn?

17 Sui saves £74. She gives $\frac{1}{8}$ of her savings to her favourite cat charity. How much money does Sui give away?

18 Boris gets £4.89 in pocket money each week. How much pocket money does Boris have after 7 weeks? Give your answer to the nearest 10p.

19 Andy hits 85% of his tennis shots on target. Jamie hits the target $\frac{27}{30}$ times. Who has the best target score?

20 What percentage of 40 is 36?

Published by Keen Kite Books
An imprint of HarperCollins*Publishers*
The News Building, 1 London Bridge Street
London SE1 9GF

ISBN 9780008161903

Text © 2015 Frances Naismith

Design © 2015 Keen Kite Books, an imprint of
HarperCollins*Publishers* Ltd

Answers

Pages 4–5

1.
> The question should invite the 'highest common factor' to be found.

 a) 3 **b)** 8 **c)** 4

2. **a)** $\frac{1}{3}$ **b)** $\frac{2}{4}$ **c)** $\frac{1}{4}$

3. **a)** 3 **b)** 2 **c)** 5

4. **a)** $\frac{2}{3}$ **b)** $\frac{5}{9}$ **c)** $\frac{2}{3}$

5. $\frac{16}{20}$ ⤫ $\frac{25}{35}$

 $\frac{5}{7}$ ⤫ $\frac{4}{5}$

 $\frac{1}{4}$ ⤫ $\frac{3}{7}$

 $\frac{18}{30}$ ⤫ $\frac{3}{5}$

 $\frac{9}{21}$ ⤫ $\frac{8}{32}$

6. Maths

7. **a)** $\frac{5}{6}$ **b)** $\frac{6}{5}$ **c)** $\frac{2}{5}$

Pages 6–7

1. **a)** $\frac{4}{8}$ **b)** $\frac{6}{8}$ **c)** $\frac{2}{8}$

2. **a)** $\frac{2}{12}$ **b)** $\frac{4}{12}$
 c) $\frac{3}{12}$ **d)** $\frac{6}{12}$

3. **a)** $\frac{4}{20}$ **b)** $\frac{2}{20}$
 c) $\frac{5}{20}$ **d)** $\frac{10}{20}$

4. **a)** $\frac{8}{16}$ **b)** $\frac{4}{16}$
 c) $\frac{6}{16}$ **d)** $\frac{14}{16}$

5. **a)** $\frac{6}{10}$ **b)** $\frac{2}{10}$
 c) $\frac{5}{10}$ **d)** $\frac{8}{10}$

6. **a)** $\frac{12}{24}$ **b)** $\frac{6}{24}$
 c) $\frac{2}{24}$ **d)** $\frac{1}{24}$

7. **a)** $\frac{8}{12}$ **b)** $\frac{3}{12}$
 c) $\frac{9}{12}$ **d)** $\frac{2}{12}$

8. **a)** $\frac{6}{8}$ **b)** $\frac{4}{8}$
 c) $\frac{3}{8}$ **d)** $\frac{4}{8}$

9. **a)** 12ths **b)** 24ths
 c) 20ths **d)** 10ths

10. **a)** $\frac{8}{12}, \frac{16}{24}$ **b)** $\frac{3}{4}, \frac{9}{12}$ **c)** $\frac{6}{18}, \frac{9}{27}, \frac{1}{3}$

Pages 8–9

1. **a)** $\frac{4}{5}$ **b)** $\frac{5}{6}$ **c)** $\frac{23}{24}$

2. **a)** $\frac{2}{3} < \frac{3}{4}$
 b) $\frac{4}{5} > \frac{2}{3}$
 c) $\frac{3}{4} < \frac{5}{6}$

3. **a)** $1\frac{3}{5} < 1\frac{2}{3}$ **b)** $2\frac{5}{8} > 2\frac{7}{12}$ **c)** $1\frac{2}{3} > 1\frac{5}{8}$

4. **a)** $\frac{5}{6}$ **b)** $\frac{6}{8}$ **c)** $\frac{5}{9}$

5. Brooklyn

6. Laiba

7. **a)** $\frac{1}{2}$ **b)** $\frac{3}{10}$ **c)** $\frac{1}{2}$

Pages 10–11

1. **a)** $\frac{1}{2}, \frac{5}{8}, \frac{3}{4}$
 b) $\frac{1}{2}, \frac{2}{3}, \frac{5}{6}$
 c) $\frac{1}{4}, \frac{2}{6}, \frac{5}{12}, \frac{2}{3}$

2. **a)** $\frac{2}{5}$ $\frac{1}{2}$ $\frac{6}{10}$
 b) $\frac{3}{16}$ $\frac{3}{8}$ $\frac{3}{4}$
 c) $\frac{6}{24}$ $\frac{4}{12}$ $\frac{5}{6}$

3. **a)** $\frac{1}{2} \frac{2}{3} \frac{3}{4} \frac{5}{6}$
 b) $\frac{2}{6} \frac{1}{2} \frac{5}{8} \frac{2}{3}$
 c) $\frac{2}{6} \frac{5}{12} \frac{2}{3} \frac{3}{4} \frac{7}{8}$

4. **a)** $\frac{1}{2}, \frac{3}{4}, \frac{11}{12}, 1\frac{3}{8}, 1\frac{5}{12}, 1\frac{2}{3}, 1\frac{5}{6}$
 b) $\frac{6}{7}, \frac{20}{21}, 1\frac{1}{3}, 1\frac{5}{14}, 1\frac{5}{6}, 2\frac{1}{2}$
 c) $\frac{7}{12}, \frac{28}{24}, \frac{6}{4}, \frac{10}{6}, \frac{14}{8}, \frac{6}{3}$

Pages 12–13

1. **a)** $\frac{7}{8}$ **b)** $\frac{3}{6}$ or $\frac{1}{2}$ **c)** $\frac{3}{10}$

2. **a)** $\frac{5}{6}$ **b)** $\frac{8}{8}$ or 1 **c)** $\frac{6}{12}$ or $\frac{1}{2}$

3. **a)** $\frac{6}{12}$ or $\frac{1}{2}$ **b)** $\frac{7}{8}$ **c)** $\frac{7}{12}$

4. **a)** $1\frac{17}{24}$ **b)** $1\frac{7}{24}$ **c)** $1\frac{7}{15}$

5. **a)** $\frac{11}{14}$ **b)** $\frac{1}{2}$ **c)** $\frac{24}{35}$

6. $\frac{59}{60}$

7. $\frac{69}{108}$ or $\frac{23}{36}$

Pages 14–15

1. **a)** $\frac{1}{4}$ **b)** $\frac{3}{8}$ **c)** $\frac{7}{20}$

2. **a)** $\frac{1}{6}$ **b)** $\frac{1}{12}$ **c)** $\frac{6}{10}$ or $\frac{3}{5}$

3. **a)** $\frac{3}{8}$ **b)** $1\frac{8}{12}$ or $1\frac{2}{3}$ **c)** $\frac{4}{12}$ or $\frac{1}{3}$
 d) $\frac{2}{12}$ or $\frac{1}{6}$ **e)** $\frac{7}{8}$ **f)** $\frac{7}{15}$

4. **a)** $\frac{1}{3}$ **b)** $\frac{1}{5}$ **c)** $\frac{1}{12}$

5. $\frac{5}{24}$

6. $\frac{9}{42}$ or $\frac{3}{14}$

Page 16

1. **a)** $\frac{1}{4}$ **b)** $\frac{1}{3}$ **c)** $\frac{1}{4}$

2. **a)** $\frac{9}{10}$ **b)** $\frac{13}{24}$ **c)** $\frac{3}{5}$

3. **a)** $\frac{2}{3}$ **b)** $\frac{2}{3}$ **c)** $\frac{1}{3}$

4. **a)** $\frac{5}{6}$ **b)** $\frac{2}{6}$ **c)** $\frac{2}{6}$

5. **a)** $\frac{3}{7}$ **b)** $\frac{16}{12}$ **c)** $\frac{14}{20}$

6. Tabitha

7. $\frac{4}{12}, \frac{1}{2}, \frac{8}{12}, \frac{3}{4}, \frac{5}{6}$

8. $\frac{7}{12}, \frac{5}{8}, \frac{4}{6}, \frac{3}{4}$

9. $\frac{19}{42}$

10. $\frac{15}{24}$ or $\frac{5}{8}$

Answers

Page 17

1. **a)** $\frac{2}{7}$ **b)** $\frac{3}{4}$ **c)** $\frac{4}{7}$

2. **a)** $\frac{6}{12}$ **b)** $\frac{1}{12}$ **c)** $\frac{2}{12}$

3. Maths

4. $\frac{2}{10}, \frac{18}{40}, \frac{3}{5}, \frac{5}{8}, \frac{14}{20}$

5. $\frac{18}{24}$ or $\frac{3}{4}$

6. $\frac{23}{30}$

7. $\frac{3}{28}$

8. $\frac{4}{15}$

9. **a)** $\frac{3}{8}$ **b)** $\frac{1}{7}$ **c)** $\frac{2}{7}$

10. 140

Pages 18–19

1. **a)** $\frac{1}{8}$ **b)** $\frac{1}{15}$ **c)** $\frac{1}{24}$

2. **a)** $\frac{6}{15}$ or $\frac{2}{5}$ **b)** $\frac{8}{21}$ **c)** $\frac{15}{24}$ or $\frac{5}{8}$

3. **a)** $\frac{5}{21}$ **b)** $\frac{15}{28}$ **c)** $\frac{21}{20}$

4. **a)** $\frac{1}{4}$ **b)** $\frac{2}{7}$ **c)** $\frac{9}{16}$

5. **a)** $\frac{24}{180}$ or $\frac{2}{15}$ **b)** $\frac{45}{192}$ or $\frac{15}{64}$ **c)** $\frac{40}{168}$ or $\frac{5}{21}$

6. **a)** $\frac{2}{3} \times \frac{4}{6} = \frac{8}{\mathbf{18}}$

    b) $\frac{2}{8} \times \frac{5}{6} = \frac{10}{48}$

    c) $\frac{5}{4} \times \frac{4}{9} = \frac{\mathbf{20}}{36}$

Pages 20–21

1. **a)** $\frac{1}{8}$ **b)** $\frac{1}{12}$ **c)** $\frac{1}{10}$

2. **a)** $\frac{1}{8}$ **b)** $\frac{1}{12}$ **c)** $\frac{1}{16}$

3. **a)** $\frac{1}{12}$ **b)** $\frac{1}{18}$ **c)** $\frac{1}{9}$

4. **a)** $\frac{1}{12}$ **b)** $\frac{1}{12}$ **c)** $\frac{1}{8}$

5. $\frac{1}{8}$

6. $\frac{1}{9}$

7. **a)** $\frac{1}{32}$ **b)** $\frac{1}{30}$ **c)** $\frac{1}{60}$

Pages 22–23

1. **a)** 3 tenths
   b) 3 thousandths
   c) 3 hundredths

2. **a)** 3.9
   b) 4.1
   c) 4.3
   d) 4.6

3. **a)** Any number with a 4 in the hundredths column
   b) Any number with a 7 in the tenths column
   c) Any number with a 2 in the thousandths column

4. **a)** 1.71
   b) 1.73
   c) 1.75
   d) 1.78

5. Numbers containing:
   a) 2.35
   b) 0.684
   c) 0.039

6. **a)** 1.052
   b) 1.054
   c) 1.056
   d) 1.059

Pages 24–25

1. **a)** 250
   b) 32
   c) 5

2. **a)** 76
   b) 740
   c) 6.2

3. **a)** 759
   b) 613
   c) 542

4. **a)** 27
   b) 34.5
   c) 95.67

5. **a)** 540
   b) 873.4
   c) 507

6. **a)** 23500
   b) 3
   c) 9540

7. **a)** 100
   b) 0.0305
   c) 0.6

8. 5456 m

9. 342 cm

Pages 26–27

1. **a)** 0.5
   b) 0.3
   c) 0.7

2. **a)** 0.43
   b) 0.86
   c) 0.52

3. **a)** 0.546
   b) 0.238
   c) 0.967

4. **a)** 68
   b) 9.5
   c) 0.048

5. **a)** 5.64
   b) 0.318
   c) 4.76

6. **a)** 5.246
   b) 2.738
   c) 4.567

7. **a)** 100
   b) 270
   c) 0.56

8. 0.0345 m or 3.45 cm

9. £45.73

Answers

Page 28

1. a) $\frac{1}{15}$ b) $\frac{1}{32}$ c) $\frac{1}{63}$
2. a) $\frac{15}{42}$ or $\frac{5}{14}$ b) $\frac{15}{28}$ c) $\frac{21}{30}$ or $\frac{7}{10}$
3. a) $\frac{1}{10}$ b) $\frac{1}{9}$ c) $\frac{1}{20}$
4. a) $\frac{1}{16}$ b) $\frac{1}{12}$ c) $\frac{1}{21}$
5. $\frac{1}{6}$
6. a) 8 hundredths
   b) 8 tenths
   c) 8 thousandths
7. a) 10
   b) 3.45
   c) 0.3
8. a) 10
   b) 360
   c) 4.39
9. a) 23 500 m
   b) 3280 cm
   c) 0.655 kg
10. 3.457 km

Page 29

1. a) $\frac{1}{5}$ b) $\frac{15}{28}$ c) $\frac{1}{3}$
2. $\frac{1}{15}$
3. a) $\frac{1}{3} \div 3 = \frac{1}{9}$
   b) $\frac{2}{4} \times \frac{3}{4} = \frac{6}{16}$
   c) $\frac{1}{4} \div 2 = \frac{1}{8}$
4. a) 1
   b) 3
   c) 7
5. a) 100
   b) 2360
   c) 0.008
6. 0.45 m
7. 325 cm
8. 0.035
9. 7895p
10. 4.63 m

Pages 30–31

1. a) 31.5
   b) 42.4
   c) 38
2. a) 21.9
   b) 27.18
   c) 40.85
3. a) 139.84
   b) 275.88
   c) 253.23
4. £183.60
5. £81.25
6. £135.45

Pages 32–33

1. a) 13
   b) 27.2
   c) 24.5
   d) 8.8
2. a) 8.25
   b) 26.25
   c) 17.25
   d) 7.25
3. a) 48.25
   b) 51.25
   c) 44.25
4. 8.25
5. 32

Pages 34–35

1. a) 0.2
   b) 0.25
   c) 0.6
   d) 0.5
   e) 0.3
   f) 0.8
2. a) 0.75
   b) 0.625
   c) 0.25
3. a) 0.375
   b) 1.75
   c) 1.125
4.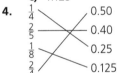

Pages 36–37

1. a) 6.3
   b) 7.3
   c) 24.8
2. a) 29
   b) 48
   c) 43
3. 21

> The question is seeking the estimated answer when 6.8 and 3.4 are each rounded to the nearest whole number, i.e. 7 × 3 = 21

4. a) 14.6
   b) 33.1
   c) 33.1
5. a) 6 km
   b) £7.00
   c) 5 m
6. 51.8 cm

Pages 38–39

1. a) 0.4
   b) 0.75
   c) 0.25

Answers

2. a) 5%
b) 2%
c) 4%

3. a) 20%
b) 90%
c) 70%

4. a) 80%
b) $\frac{32}{100}$ or $\frac{8}{25}$
c) 45%

5. a) 30% < $\frac{12}{20}$
b) 0.125 = $\frac{1}{8}$
c) $\frac{8}{24}$ < 35%

6. Gina

Page 40

1. 31.05
2. £89.96
3. £4.80
4. 18.6
5. a) 0.75
b) 0.75
c) 0.25
6. 0.01 $\frac{6}{8}$
0.50 $\frac{3}{24}$
0.75 $\frac{1}{100}$
0.125 $\frac{12}{24}$
7. 30.1
8. 23

> There is no need to round the answer to one decimal place as stated in the question.

9. 80% = 0.8 = $\frac{80}{100}$ = $\frac{8}{10}$ or equivalents
10. Harry 75%

Page 41

1. 275.4
2. £89.40
3. 21.75
4. 18.25
5. 0.625
6. 22.14
7. 190
8. Maths 64%
9. 12.5%   0.035
0.35 $\frac{3}{12}$
25% $\frac{70}{200}$
$\frac{35}{1000}$ 0.125
10. 25% = 0.25 = $\frac{25}{100}$ = $\frac{1}{4}$

Pages 42–43

1. a) $\frac{7}{20}$
b) $\frac{3}{7}$
c) $\frac{2}{15}$

2. a) $\frac{18}{24}$, $\frac{20}{24}$, $\frac{21}{24}$

3. a) 0.25
b) $\frac{7}{10}$
c) 0.3

4. $\frac{1}{2}$, $\frac{7}{12}$, $\frac{2}{3}$, $\frac{3}{4}$, $\frac{5}{6}$
5. $\frac{45}{30}$ or $\frac{3}{2}$ or $1\frac{1}{2}$
6. $\frac{1}{4}$ + $\frac{3}{8}$ = $\frac{5}{8}$
7. $\frac{7}{12}$
8. $\frac{2}{24}$ or $\frac{1}{12}$
9. $\frac{1}{15}$
10. $\frac{1}{8}$
11. $2\frac{4}{11}$ + $\frac{3}{11}$ = $2\frac{7}{11}$
12. 0.875
13. 2 thousandths
14. 7
15. 54.3
16. £105
17. £9.25
18. £34.20
19. Jamie 90%
20. 90%